We would like to thank the following people for their contributions:

    Caroline Bergeron- Cover photo
    Lauren Brownstein- make up
    Brittney & Brooke Udall- food display and baking
    Luc Meilleur- food photographer

Copyright © 2017 99 Series, LLC
All rights reserved. No part of this publication may be reproduced, distributed, or transmitted in any form or by any means, including photocopying, recording, or other electronic or mechanical methods, without the prior written permission of the publisher, except in the case of brief quotations embodied in critical reviews and certain other noncommercial uses permitted by copyright law. For permission requests, write to the publisher, addressed "Attention: Permissions" at info at kidswritenetwork.com

#smartbites

Foreword

When you get to a certain point in your life, you want to share your healthy lifestyle with your family, your friends and with everyone you know. I have trained for over 15 years and it is a part of my lifestyle. I never let a day go by without some type of physical exercise.

Four years ago, I wrote a children's book that promotes child mental health. I had the opportunity to visit many schools and speak to children about their daily challenges. Through my book tour, I realized that the time I was taking to promote child mental health could also be a chance for me to promote physical health starting with food! When I first began my training with Renée, she would bring me homemade snacks and insist that I eat them after my workout. Growing up, I always felt that the snacks sold in grocery stores were unhealthy so I became a "non-snack" person.

Slowly I began to incorporate snacks into my daily routine. Renée would pop snacks into my mouth (literally) to taste test them. They were delicious and they actually boosted my energy. I would never have thought to eat snacks after my workouts.

During one of my workouts, as I was finishing a set of lunges, it hit me! Why not create a cookbook using Renée's recipes that can offer parents a healthy alternative for their children and for themselves! These snacks were fast, easy to make, tasted great AND healthy! They passed the test with my 5 kids so why not make a cookbook that caters to the fast paced world we live in today.

One by one, Renée would make her recipes with me so I could understand exactly what she kept telling me all these years. It took us under one hour to make 3 recipes! Whether you have a family of 5 or whether you're a single mom with one child, the time it takes to make these recipes is irrelevant.

I witnessed them being made, taste tested them first hand and I am able to say that this cookbook will change the way you look at chocolate!

You just can't tell what is in them! Renée has done a fabulous job in personalizing these wonderful recipes that offer so many health benefits for your children.

I started making them for my family, and my kids not only ask for these snacks, they also have no idea that they are eating their veggies! Who would have guessed that black beans could turn into chocolate brownies!

While I am an advocate for youth mental health, I truly believe that eating healthy can only help promote a balanced lifestyle for both children and adults alike.

After all, the greatest wealth is mental health!

Maria Guzzo

Table of contents

1. Smoothies

2. Energy balls

3. Treats

4. Cookies

5. Muffins

6. Bread

7. Overnight Oats

SMOOTHIES

Ruby Red Smoothie

INGREDIENTS :

- 1 beet
- 1 carrot
- 1 orange
- 1 cup of strawberries
- 8 oz. of water

INTRUCTIONS :

1. Add ingredients into blender. Mix it until smooth
2. Chill

Renée: A good "pick me up" when your energy is low!

Good Morning Smoothie

INGREDIENTS :

- 1 pink grapefruit
- 1 cup of strawberries
- 1 cup of kale
- 8 oz. of water

INSTRUCTIONS :

1. Add ingredients into blender. Mix it until smooth
2. Chill

Renée: Refreshing!

My Little Genius Smoothie

INGREDIENTS :

- 1 cup of blueberries
- 1 cup of spinach
- Pinch of ginger
- 8 oz. of water

INSTRUCTIONS :

1. Add ingredients into blender. Mix it until smooth
2. Drink immediately

Renée: Great during exams!

Tropical Smoothie

INGREDIENTS :

- 1 banana
- 1 cup of pineapple chunks
- 1 cup of baby spinach
- 8 oz. of liquid (orange juice or water)

INSTRUCTIONS :

1. Add ingredients into blender. Mix it until smooth
2. Chill

Renée: My son's favorite 1 hour before a big hockey game!

Recovery Smoothie

INGREDIENTS :

- 1 cup of pumpkin puree
- 1 banana
- 1 tsp cinnamon
- 8 oz. of almond milk

INSTRUCTIONS :

1. Add ingredients into blender. Mix it until smooth
2. Chill

Renée: Great when those muscles ache after a hard work out.

Sunshine Smoothie

INGREDIENTS :

- 8 oz. of almond milk
- 1 banana
- ½ cup of mango chunks
- ½ cup of pineapple chunks
- ½ yellow pepper diced
- ¼ cup of shredded coconut

INSTRUCTIONS :

1. Add ingredients into blender. Mix it until smooth
2. Chill

ENERGY BALLS

Fig and Walnut Energy Balls

Recipe for 12 balls

INGREDIENTS :

- ¼ cup of dates
- 1 cup of figs
- 1 ½ tbsp of maple syrup
- 1 tbsp of water
- 1 cup of walnuts
- 1 tsp of anise

INSTRUCTIONS :

1. Chop nuts into small pieces using a food processor
2. Add other ingredients and blend
3. Wet hands and shape balls
4. Freeze for 20 mins

Maria: European twist to North American healthy eating habits.

Energy Chocolate Balls

Recipe for 12 balls

INGREDIENTS :

- 1 cup of walnuts
- ¾ cup of dates
- ¼ cup of cacao
- 2 tbsp of maple syrup
- Pinch of salt

INSTRUCTIONS :

1. Chop walnuts into small pieces using a food processor
2. Add other ingredients and blend
3. Wet hands hand shape balls
4. Freeze 20 mins

Peanut Butter Protein Balls

Recipe for 8 balls

INGREDIENTS :

- ½ cup of almond milk
- 1 cup of peanut butter
- 1 tbsp of honey
- 1 ½ cups of protein powder
- 2 cups of oats

INSTRUCTIONS :

1. Mix ingredients together
2. Wet hands and shape balls
3. Freeze for 20 mins

Crispy Energy Balls

Recipe for 8 balls

INGREDIENTS :

- ¼ cup of sunflower seed butter
- 3 tbsp of maple syrup
- 1 tsp of vanilla extract
- 1 cup of rice crispy cereal
- ¼ cup of dark chocolate chips

INSTRUCTIONS :

1. Mix ingredients together
2. Wet hands and shape balls
3. Freeze for 20 mins

Apricot Almond Energy Balls

Recipe for 12 balls

INGREDIENTS :

- ½ cup of almonds
- 1 cup of apricots
- ¼ cup of dates
- 2 tbsp of almond butter
- 2 tbsp of shredded coconut
- 1 tsp of vanilla extract
- Pinch of salt

INSTRUCTIONS :

1. Chop almonds into small pieces using a food processor
2. Add other ingredients and process
3. Wet hands and shape balls
4. Freeze 20 mins

TREATS

Sweet Potato Brownies

Recipe for 24 mini bites

INGREDIENTS :

- 1 sweet potato baked and pilled (about 1 cup)
- ¼ cup of coconut oil
- ⅓ cup of maple syrup
- ½ cup of cacao powder
- 2 eggs
- ⅓ cup of dark chocolate chips
- 24 walnuts halves

INSTRUCTIONS :

1. Preheat oven at 350
2. Add sweet potato, maple syrup and eggs to food processor and blend until smooth
3. Melt coconut oil in microwave, about 60 seconds.
4. Add coconut oil and cacao powder to food processor and blend until smooth.
5. Add chocolate chips and mix with spatula
6. Grease mini muffin tin with coconut oil
7. Place batter in tin
8. Place walnut on top of each one
9. Bake for 20 mins

Maria: Having never baked healthy snacks from scratch before, especially sweet potato brownies, I have to say I was tempted to lick the spoon

Bounty Bites

INGREDIENTS :

- 2 cups of dark chocolate chips
- 1 cup of almonds
- ½ cup of roasted shredded coconut

INSTRUCTIONS :

1. Preheat oven at 400 degrees
2. Place parchment paper on cookie sheet
3. Chop almonds into big pieces and place them on cookie sheet, bake at 400 for 10 minutes
4. Toast coconut in a frying pan until golden brown
5. Add chocolate chips over almonds then bake for 2 minutes
6. Use spatula to coat nuts with melted chocolate and add toasted coconut
7. Chill in freezer for about 30 minutes
8. Break into pieces

Maria: Prepared these in between packing my son's fencing bag and getting him in the car

Black Bean Brownies

Recipe for 24 mini bites

INGREDIENTS :

- 2 cups oat flour (Blend oats in food processor for 2 minutes)
- 1 cup of black beans
- 1 cup of pumpkin puree (canned or cooked)
- 1 cup of cacao
- 3 eggs
- 1 tsp salt
- ¾ tsp baking soda
- 1 tsp vanilla extract
- 1 tbsp of coconut oil (melted)
- 1 cup of dark chocolate chips

INSTRUCTIONS :

1. Preheat oven at 350 degrees
2. Process wet ingredients (Black beans, pumpkin, eggs and coconut oil) and transfer into a bowl.
3. Mix in dry ingredients
4. Grease mini muffin tin
5. Bake at 350 for 30 minutes

Renée: I like to cook dried beans in slow cooker for 10 hours and then freeze them by portions.

Raw Date Squares

INGREDIENTS CRUST :

- 1 ½ cup of almonds
- 1 ½ cup of oats
- Pinch of salt
- 10 dates
- ¼ cup of coconut oil (melt in microwave about 40 seconds)

INGREDIENTS FILLING:

- 25 dates
- ¼ cup of water

INSTRUCTIONS :

1. Line square pan with parchment paper
2. Process almonds, oats and salt in food processor
3. Add 10 dates and melted coconut oil
4. Place ¾ of mixture in pan
5. Process filling using food processor
6. Add to pan
7. Spread remaining crust over filling
8. Pat down and refrigerate

Renée: These are great when you do not have time to bake!

COOKIES

Oat Banana Cookies

Recipe for 8 cookies

INGREDIENTS :

- 2 ripe bananas
- 2 cups of Quick Oats
- ¼ cup of chocolate chip
- 1 tsp of vanilla extract
- 1 tsp of cinnamon

INSTRUCTIONS :

1. Preheat oven at 350
2. Line a cookie sheet with parchment paper
3. Mash the bananas
4. Add other ingredients and mix well
5. Shape cookies
6. Bake for 10 minutes

Maria: Making these cookies with simple directions has made me forget about packaged cookies for my kids.

Renée: Don't throw out those extra ripe bananas! They make cookies your kids will approve!

Pear and Walnut Oat Cookies

Recipe for 8 cookies

INGREDIENTS :

- 2 pears
- 2 tbsp of honey
- ¼ cup of water
- ½ tsp of cinnamon
- ½ tsp of vanilla extract
- 1 tsp of coconut oil (microwave about 20 seconds)
- 2 cups of oats (I prefer quick oats for this recipe)
- ¼ cup of chopped walnuts

INSTRUCTIONS :

1. Preheat oven at 350 degrees
2. Chop pears and bring to a boil with water
3. Add cinnamon, vanilla and melted coconut oil and let boil until pears are soft about 5 minutes
4. Add remaining ingredients and mix until well blended. Shape cookies
5. Bake at 350 for 10 minutes

Maria: You never know who will knock at your door for a last minute visit. Quick, easy and delicious.

Double Chocolate Protein Cookies

Recipe for 6 cookies

INGREDIENTS :

- 1 cup of Quick oats
- ½ cup of protein powder
- 1 egg
- ¼ cup of nature peanut butter
- 1 ½ tbsp of cacao
- 2 tbsp of honey
- ¼ cup of dark chocolate chips

INSTRUCTIONS :

1. Preheat oven at 350 degrees
2. Place peanut butter and honey in a pot, melt and then add other ingredients. Mix well
3. Shape cookies and place on parchment paper
4. Bake at 350 for 10 mins

Maria: A healthy way of eating chocolate without feeling guilty!

Black Bean Chocolate Cookies

Recipe for 12 cookies

INGREDIENTS :

- 2 cups of black bean (canned or cooked)
- 2 tbsp of olive oil
- 1 egg
- 2 tsp of vanilla extract
- 2 tbsp of almond milk
- ½ cup of pumpkin puree
- ¼ cup of brown sugar
- ¼ cup of cacao
- 1 tsp of baking powder
- ¼ tsp of cinnamon
- 2 tbsp of grounded flaxseed
- 2 tbsp of spelt flour

INSTRUCTIONS :

1. Preheat oven at 350 degrees
2. Place all ingredients in food processor and blend until smooth
3. Grease cookie sheet with coconut oil
4. Bake at 350 for 10 minutes

Maria: My son still does not know there are black beans in these.

Oatmeal Chocolate Chip Cookies

Recipe for 12 cookies

INGREDIENTS :

- 2 cups of oat flour (Blend oats in food processor for 2 minutes)
- 1 tsp of baking powder
- 1 tsp of cinnamon
- Pinch of salt
- 2 eggs
- 1 ¼ cup of chickpeas
- 2 ripe bananas
- ½ cup of brown sugar
- 2 tsp of vanilla extract
- ½ cup of dark chocolate chips

INSTRUCTIONS :

1. Preheat oven at 375 degrees
2. Place wet ingredients in food processor and blend until smooth.
3. Transfer into bowl and add dry ingredients. Mix well
4. Grease cookie sheet with coconut oil
5. Bake at 375 for 12 mins

Maria: Good-bye pre-wrapped store bought cookies! Hello fresh and healthy!

Renée: I had my 14-year-old son make them…his reaction was: that was easy!

MUFFINS

Red Velvet Healthy Style

Recipe for 12 muffins

INGREDIENTS :

- 1 ⅓ cups of oat flour (blend in food processor for 2 minutes)
- ½ cup of cacao
- 3 tsp of baking powder
- Pinch of salt
- 1 cup of cooked beets
- 2 eggs
- ¼ cup of maple syrup
- ⅓ cup of brown sugar
- ¼ cup of black beans
- ¼ cup of almond milk
- ½ cup of dark chocolate chips

INSTRUCTIONS :

1. Preheat oven at 375 degrees
2. Grease muffin tin with coconut oil or use muffin papers
3. In a medium bowl, combine oat flour, cacao, baking powder and salt
4. Add wet ingredients to food processor and blend until smooth
5. Add dry ingredients to food processor and blend.
6. Add chocolate chips and mix with spatula
7. I like to make 6 jumbo muffins, bake 20 minutes

Maria: Too busy licking the bowl I forgot to put them in the oven.

Renée: They won't believe the muffin is healthy, they will insist it's a cupcake.

Butternut Squash Carrot Apple Muffins

Recipe for 12 muffins

INGREDIENTS :

- 2 cups of oat flour (blend in food processor for 2 minutes)
- ⅓ cup of brown sugar
- 3 tsp of baking powder
- ¾ tsp of salt
- 1 tsp of cinnamon
- 1 tsp of vanilla extract
- ⅓ cup of chickpeas
- 1 egg
- 1 cup of almond milk
- 1 cup of grated carrots
- 1 cup of cooked butternut squash
- ½ cup of pumpkin seeds
- 1 apple diced

INSTRUCTIONS :

1. Preheat oven at 350
2. Cut butternut squash and boil with peel. Remove peel once cooked
3. Grease muffin tin with coconut oil or use muffin papers
4. Blend chickpeas, eggs, almond milk and squash in food processor
5. Transfer to bowl and add remaining ingredients. Mix well
6. Cook for 20 minutes

Renée: For those of you who aren't chocolate lovers

Blueberry Muffins

Recipe for 12 muffins

INGREDIENTS :

- 2 cups of oat flour (blend oats in food processor for 2 minutes)
- ¼ cup of maple syrup
- ½ mashed banana
- ½ tsp of salt
- 2 tsp of baking powder
- ⅓ cup of chickpeas
- 1 egg
- ⅓ cup of almond milk
- 1 cup of blueberries
- 1 tsp of Cinnamon

INSTRUCTIONS :

1. Preheat oven at 350 degrees
2. Grease muffin tin with coconut oil or use muffin papers
3. Blend egg, chickpeas and almond milk in food processor until smooth
4. Transfer into a bowl and add remaining ingredients. Mix well
5. Cook 20 minutes

Zucchini Bran Muffins

Recipe for 12 muffins

INGREDIENTS :

- 1 ½ cups of oat flour (blend in food processor for 2 minutes)
- 1 ½ cups of bran
- ½ cup of brown sugar
- 1 tbsp of cinnamon
- 1 tsp of baking powder
- 1 tsp of baking soda
- Pinch salt
- 1 cup of dried raisins
- 1 cup of grated zucchini
- 1 ¾ cups of almond milk
- ¼ cup of chickpeas
- 1 egg

INSTRUCTIONS :

1. Preheat oven at 400 degrees.
2. Grease muffin tin with coconut oil or use muffin papers
3. Process last 3 ingredients in food processor until smooth
4. Transfer into bowl and mix in other ingredients
5. Bake at 400 for 20 minutes

Cranberry Orange Muffins

Recipe for 12 muffins

INGREDIENTS :

- 2 cups of oat flour (blend oats in food processor for 2 minutes)
- ¼ cup of maple syrup
- ½ mashed banana
- ½ tsp of salt
- 2 tsp of baking powder
- ⅓ cup of chickpeas
- 1 egg
- ⅓ cup of orange juice (about 1 orange freshly squeezed)
- 1 cup of cranberries
- 1 tsp of vanilla extract
- Zest of 1 orange

INSTRUCTIONS :

1. Preheat oven at 350 degrees
2. Grease muffin tin with coconut oil or use muffin papers
3. Blend egg, chickpeas, banana and orange juice in food processor until smooth
4. Transfer into a bowl and add remaining ingredients. Mix well
5. Cook 20 minutes

Raspberries and Coconut Muffins

Recipe for 12 muffins

INGREDIENTS :

- 2 cups of oat flour (blend oats in food processor for 2 minutes)
- ¼ cup of maple syrup
- ½ tsp of salt
- 2 tsp of baking powder
- ⅓ cup of chickpeas
- 1 egg
- ⅓ cup of coconut milk
- 1 cup of raspberries
- ¼ cup of grilled shredded coconut

INSTRUCTIONS :

1. Preheat oven at 350 degrees
2. Grease muffin tin with coconut oil or use muffin papers
3. Blend egg, chickpeas and coconut milk in food processor until smooth
4. Transfer into a bowl and add remaining ingredients. Mix well
5. Cook 20 minutes

Protein Oat Banana Chocolate Chip Muffins

Recipe for 12 muffins

INGREDIENTS :

- 1 banana mashed
- 2 eggs
- ½ cup of greek yogourt
- ¾ cup of oats
- 2 scoops of protein powder
- ¼ cup of brown sugar (not required if using flavored protein)
- 1 tsp of baking powder
- 1 tsp of baking soda
- ½ cup of chocolate chips

INSTRUCTIONS :

1. Preheat oven at 350 degree
2. Place all ingredients in food processor and blend until smooth
3. Grease muffin tin with coconut oil or use muffin papers
4. Bake at 350 for 20 minutes

BREAD

Zucchini Bread

INGREDIENTS :

- 2 cups of oat Flour (blend in food processor for 2 minutes)
- 1 cup of grated zucchini
- 3 eggs
- Pinch of salt
- ⅓ cup of chickpeas
- 1 banana mashed
- 2 tbsp of maple syrup
- 1 tsp of cinnamon
- 2 tsp of baking powder
- ½ cup of raisins

INSTRUCTIONS :

1. Preheat oven at 350 degrees
2. Grease bread tin with coconut oil
3. Add chickpeas, eggs, banana and maple syrup to food processor and blend until smooth
4. Put dry ingredients in a bowl and add wet ones mix well
5. Cook for 60 minutes or 25 minutes if mini breads

Quinoa Banana Bread

INGREDIENTS :

- 2 cups of cooked quinoa
- 1 cup of rice flour
- ⅔ cup of brown sugar
- ½ cup of chickpeas
- 3 eggs
- 1 tsp of vanilla
- 1 tsp of cinnamon
- 1 ¼ tsp of baking soda
- Pinch salt
- 2 mashed bananas
- ½ cup of dark chocolate chips

INSTRUCTIONS :

1. Preheat oven at 350 degrees
2. Add eggs, chickpeas and vanilla to food processor and blend until smooth
3. Transfer to bowl and mix in other ingredients
4. Grease bread tin with coconut oil
5. Bake at 350 for 1 hour or 25 minutes if using miniature bread tin

Carrot and Walnut Bread

INGREDIENTS :

- 2 cups of oat Flour (blend in food processor for 2 minutes)
- 1 cup of grated carrots
- 3 eggs
- Pinch of salt
- ⅓ cup of chickpeas
- ¼ cup of maple syrup
- 1 tsp of cinnamon
- 2 tsps of baking powder
- ½ cup of raisins
- ½ cup of chopped walnuts

INSTRUCTIONS :

1. Preheat oven at 350 degrees
2. Grease bread tin with coconut oil
3. Add chickpeas, eggs and maple syrup to food processor and blend until smooth
4. Mix dry and wet ingredients in a bowl, mix well
5. Cook for 60 minutes or 25 minutes if mini breads

Quinoa Chocolate Pumpkin Bread

INGREDIENTS :

- 2 cups of cooked quinoa
- 1 cup of pumpkin puree
- ½ cup of chickpeas
- 2 eggs
- ½ cup of brown sugar
- 1 tsp of vanilla extract
- ¼ cup of almond milk
- 2 tsp of baking soda
- Pinch of salt
- ½ cup of cacao
- ½ cup of dark chocolate chips
- Extra chips for decoration.

INSTRUCTIONS :

1. Preheat oven at 350 degrees
2. Add eggs, chickpeas, pumpkin puree, brown sugar, vanilla and almond milk to food processor and blend until smooth
3. Transfer to bowl and mix in other ingredients
4. Grease bread tin with coconut oil
5. Pour into bread tin and decorate with chocolate chips
6. Bake at 350 for 1 hour or 25 minutes if using miniature bread tin

Quinoa Lemon Bread

INGREDIENTS :

- 2 cups of cooked quinoa
- ⅔ cup of brown sugar
- ½ cup of chickpeas
- 3 eggs
- 1 tsp of vanilla extract
- 4 tbsp of lemon juice (about ½ of a lemon)
- 2 tsp of baking soda
- Pinch salt
- Zest of 1 lemon
- Lemon slices

INSTRUCTIONS :

1. Preheat oven at 350 degrees
2. Add eggs, chickpeas and vanilla to food processor and blend until smooth
3. Transfer to bowl and mix in other ingredients
4. Grease bread tin with coconut oil
5. Transfer dough in baking tin and add a slice of lemon for decoration
6. Bake at 350 for 1 hour or 25 minutes if using miniature bread tin

OVERNIGHT OATS

Goji Overnight Oats

INGREDIENTS :

- ¼ cup of ats
- 1 tsp of chia seeds
- 1 tsp of grounded flax seeds
- 1 cup of almond milk
- 1 tbsp of dried goji berries
- ½ tsp of vanilla extract

INSTRUCTIONS :

1. Place ingredients in a container and refrigerate overnight

Chunky Monkey Overnight Oats

INGREDIENTS :

- ¼ cup of oats
- 1 tsp of chia seeds
- 1 tsp of ground flaxseed
- 1 cup of coconut milk
- 1 tbsp of coconut flakes
- 1 tbsp of chocolate chips
- ½ banana sliced

INSTRUCTIONS :

1. Place ingredients in a container and refrigerate overnight

Apple Pie Overnight Oats

INGREDIENTS :

- ¼ cup of oats
- 1 tsp of chia seeds
- 1 tsp of ground flaxseed
- 1 cup of almond milk
- ½ apple chopped
- ½ tsp of vanilla extract
- ½ tsp of cinnamon

INSTRUCTIONS :

1. Place ingredients in a container and refrigerate overnight

Maple Walnut Overnight Oats

INGREDIENTS :

- ¼ cup of oats
- 1 tsp of chia seeds
- 1 tsp of ground flaxseed
- 1 cup of almond milk
- 2 tbsp of maple syrup
- 2 tbsp of chopped walnuts

INSTRUCTIONS :

1. Place ingredients in a container and refrigerate overnight

Banana Almond Butter Overnight Oats

INGREDIENTS :

- ¼ cup of oats
- 1 tsp of chia seeds
- 1 tsp of ground flaxseed
- 1 cup of almond milk
- 1 tbsp of almond butter
- ½ tsp of vanilla extract
- ½ banana mashed

INSTRUCTIONS :

1. Place ingredients in a container and refrigerate overnight

In 2015, Maria F. Guzzo wrote and published a children's book titled *How to Train your Dreams* as her interest in youth mental health evolved through her philanthropy. Her shift towards youth mental health began in the last few years when she became aware of the *Kids Write Network (KWN)*. Maria decided to adopt the 6-step concept as she was completing her manuscript to better understand how this initiative is implemented. Maria's involvement in her philanthropy is 100% hands-on.

Maria has taken the *Kids Write Network (KWN)* intervention to the Jewish General Hospital's Psychiatry department as a research project. This 6-step literary and therapeutic child mental health initiative is implemented in classrooms to guide students through current or past challenges.

This initiative has now become her focus as she completes her Masters Sc. in Psychiatry at McGill University. Her intention is to pursue a PhD in the department of Psychiatry in mental health research.

Since 2014, Maria has won numerous awards and been acknowledged as a leader in building awareness to youth mental health. Through her involvement, she has gained recognition as an advocate for mental health and for inspiring many to allow a conversation that reduces the stigma associated to mental health.

During her book tour in 2016, Maria felt the need to establish a connection between mental health and physical health. Her new book aptly titled #smartbites combines her philanthropy with smart and healthy snacking.

Maria's goal is to combine her philanthropic mission in youth mental health with her studies. Her short term goal within the next 5 years is to collaborate with the Minister of Education to incorporate mental health initiatives as part of school curricula across the country.

Maria's commitment to a healthy lifestyle includes regular physical activity with her children as well as encouraging their individual development in sports. Maria has a passion for photography, enjoys traveling and has an appreciation for music from the 60's and 70's.

Maria lives in Terrebonne, Québec, Canada with her husband and 5 children.

Renée Brault is a full time osteopath who worked as a personal trainer from the age of 18. She went further into the world of fitness by acquiring a Bachelor of Science in Physical Education. At a young age, she was very athletic playing every sport. During her CEGEP she began working in gyms, which would become her calling into her adult years. As a personal trainer for over 28 years, she delved into the world of osteopathy after tearing her Achilles. But that wasn't enough. Fitness was her lifestyle but she felt the need to incorporate a healthy food lifestyle into her already active world.

That would come when her son was nine years. Fed up with unhealthy snacks that she would find in grocery stores she decided to go about researching healthier snacks online. The recipes she found were great health wise but their taste did not pass her son's taste test! Determined to make sure that her son would never eat a store bought snack again, Renée began experimenting and personalizing the recipes she felt would best suit her son's taste.

Fast-forward to today, she now has 37 recipes that are not only healthy, they taste delicious! They are recipes that have been mastered over the last 4 years and tested by her son. He has never detected any of the ingredients that go into the recipes and we aren't telling him! Renée always tells her son that she can make any desert he wants and quietly smiles knowing there are plenty of veggies!

In 2014, Renée began training Maria Guzzo at the same time that Maria began her transition into youth mental health.

Today Renée operates her full time private practice since 2009 and is excited to be able to share her passion of healthy snacks. Her hope is to promote these recipes and make them available to schools.

Renée lives with her husband and son in Terrebonne, Québec, Canada.

References

http://link.springer.com/article/10.1007/s00127-012-0623-5

Please note that all recipes unless otherwise specified should be refrigerated.

CPSIA information can be obtained at www.ICGtesting.com
Printed in the USA
LVIW01n2135210417
531741LV00004B/5